ADVANCE PRAISE FOR
DOG AT THE TINSEL TREE

"How much do we love our dogs? How have our lives changed because we shared them with a pet? Denise answers these questions in her heartwarming childhood reflection in *Dog at the Tinsel Tree—Susie's Story*. The undeniable bond she shares with Susie takes us all to that place in childhood where our best buddy was a stable source of friendship, comfort, tears, and laughter. Denise has the gift of storytelling that brings us with her on her amazing journey with Susie. I could literally feel every moment. If you have not yet experienced life with a pet, please adopt a rescue animal and enrich your life!"

-**Debi Boies**
Founder/President Pilots N Paws

"Once again, this author reminds us of the power of the human-animal bond and shows us the value pets have on children and their families. This book is a must-have for all of us that have had that one special furry friend."

-**Alex Rensing, DVM**

"*Dog at the Tinsel Tree* will refresh memories of anyone's childhood pet and the adventures shared. Denise relives her childhood experiences with her best friend through the eyes of a little girl. This is not just a book to enjoy during the holidays, but a cheerful story to enjoy throughout the year."

-**Alysia Dubriske**
Liz E's Pekingese Rescue

"Denise Lee Branco delivers excellence once again with her latest animal tale, *Dog at the Tinsel Tree—Susie's Story*. She immerses readers into descriptive scenes to help them experience early life on a farm with her four-legged sibling, Susie. Funny, thoughtful, and introspective, this book is a wonderful read for anyone who enjoys nostalgia and understands the love and bond of a special pet."

-Valerie Ormond
Multiple-Award Winning Author of
The *Believing In Horses* Series

Author Denise Lee Branco has given her readers yet another heartwarming and delightful tale of what it truly means to bond with an animal. Her deep love and connection are felt throughout the entire story. It captures what all animal lovers feel and won't forget when bonding with a beloved pet."

-Dana Cotta
Lifelong Animal Lover

"I loved *Dog at the Tinsel Tree*! I, too, had a Susie. Her name was China Girl - a black and white Pekingese. She was my everything for 18 years. Saying goodbye is so hard for me. I always remember the Garth Brooks' song, 'The Dance' about me missing all the pain, but then I would have missed the dance which was wonderful. It's so personal for me to share your story of love and loss and bring the dance card full circle by helping another pet who needs me."

-Janice O'Connor
Rescued Pets are Wonderful Pekingese Rescue

"Reading this delightful story brought back memories of my first dog, a Pekingese, of my family, and holidays throughout my childhood and beyond. This is a lovely read, and it brought smiles of recognition throughout the story."

-P.L. Clark
Author of *A Time for Love*

"*Dog at the Tinsel Tree—Susie's Story* unwraps the gift of a heaven-sent puppy, bathing a child in earthly comfort and delight, spotlighting the wisdom of adopting a pet."

-June Gillam
Award-Winning Author of *Kiki's New Home*

"*Dog at the Tinsel Tree* is fantastic! The chapters were good, the characters were well expressed, and Susie, the dog, is awesome. When Branco shared that kids in middle school made fun of her for being overweight, and she'd tell Susie as soon as she got home from school, I was reminded of my own childhood. It was hard at the time, but we both rose above the emotional pain with a dog by our side."

-Diane Ponzo
Canine Angels for Heaven - A Hospice Pet Sanctuary

"This sweet story, filled with nostalgia for a simpler time, will touch dog lovers and remind them of that 'magic' of a first, beloved best friend. A short, sweet read recommended for dog lovers of any age."

-Amy Shojai
Award-Winning Author of 35+ Pet Titles including *Chicken Soup for the Dog Lover's Soul*

"In the tradition of Lassie and Dorothy's Toto, *Dog at the Tinsel Tree* welcomes all readers to the charming tale of best friends, Susie and Denise, growing up together in rural California during a slower time. From start to finish, this is an absolute page turner many of us long to find. You will enjoy countless adventures, meeting memorable characters like a loving grandmother called Ava, Duckie the duck, a feisty campground squirrel, and visualize a magical treehouse called Pine Castle, or laugh at the humorous interaction with a young farm friend called Brownie. You will learn about life on a farm through the eyes of a young girl and her fur sister, Susie. It is an adventure well worth your time and will make a lasting memory. And I wouldn't be surprised if it ended up on the big screen someday. Enjoy."

-**Pat Wright**
Poet and Storyteller

Dog at the Tinsel Tree

Susie's Story

Copyright 2023 by Denise Lee Branco

Website: www.deniseinspiresyou.com
X (formerly Twitter) & Instagram: @deniseleebranco
Facebook: DeniseInspiresYou
LinkedIn: denise-lee-branco-27309824/

All rights reserved. No part of this publication may be reproduced, stored in retrieval system, or transmitted in any form or by any means—electronic, mechanical, recording, photocopy, scanning or otherwise—except for brief quotations in critical articles and reviews, without the prior permission of the author.

Limit of Liability/Disclaimer of Warranty: While the publisher and author have used their best efforts in preparing this book, they make no representations or warranties with respect to the accuracy or completeness of the contents of this book and specifically disclaim any implied warranties of merchantability or fitness for a particular purpose. No warranty may be created or extended by sales representatives or written sales materials. The advice and strategies contained herein may not be suitable for your situation. You should consult with a professional when appropriate. Neither the publisher nor the author shall be liable for any loss of profit or any other commercial damages, including but not limited to special, incidental, consequential, personal or other damages.

All internet addresses, phone numbers, company or product information, etc. in this book are offered as a resource. They are not intended in any way to be or imply an endorsement by the author or publisher, nor does the author or publisher vouch for the content of these resources for the life of this book. The names of certain individuals have been changed to protect their privacy.

Dog at the Tinsel Tree: Susie's Story

Published by Strolling Hills Publishing, LLC
P.O. Box 674
Lincoln, CA 95648

Book cover/interior/eBook design by the Book Cover Whisperer:
OpenBookDesign.biz

Library of Congress Control Number: 2023918359

PET010000   PETS / Essays & Narratives
PET004000   PETS / Dogs / General
REL012170   RELIGION / Christian Living / Personal Memoirs

978-0-9845888-6-2 Paperback
978-0-9845888-4-8 Hardcover
978-0-9845888-5-5 eBook

FIRST EDITION

Dog
at the
Tinsel Tree

Susie's Story

Denise Lee Branco

Strolling Hills Publishing

This book is dedicated to
my parents, grandmother, and one very special dog -
four blessings who brought a little magic to
my childhood every single day.

CONTENTS

Introduction ♦ ♦ ♦ i

Holiday Traditions ♦ ♦ ♦ 1

Silver Branches ♦ ♦ ♦ 7

Priceless Gifts ♦ ♦ ♦ 15

True Obedience ♦ ♦ ♦ 23

Dance Partners ♦ ♦ ♦ 31

Mighty Protector ♦ ♦ ♦ 37

Sweet Dreams ♦ ♦ ♦ 43

Squirrel vs. Canine ♦ ♦ ♦ 47

Bicycling Buddies ♦ ♦ ♦ 53

Pine Castle ♦ ♦ ♦ 59

Getaways & Risk-Takers ♦ ♦ ♦ 65

Rise Above ♦ ♦ ♦ 71

Christmas Spirit ♦ ♦ ♦ 77

Love Letter ♦ ♦ ♦ 83

About the Author ♦ ♦ ♦ 87

Acknowledgments ♦ ♦ ♦ 89

Resources ♦ ♦ ♦ 93

INTRODUCTION

Retrospection allows us to recognize the glorious gift of a first pet. We counted on that pet for companionship and unconditional love, and it always delivered.

If blessed, we will have many pets throughout our lifetimes; but there's no question the first one will always have a special place in our hearts. And if we are blessed with our first pet in childhood, its presence will teach us many developmental lessons and help shape our futures.

My prayer is that Susie's story, about my first pet, will bring you joy and longing for the simpler times of childhood, recalling fond memories of your first pet with a newfound understanding of why it came into your life. I believe first pets are heaven-sent, arriving precisely on time—chosen for us—not by us.

Perhaps you have a desire to share your life with a pet for the first time but are uncertain whether you should take on that responsibility. My wish is that the devoted friendship Susie and I shared will show you the power of the human-animal bond, and the impact it can have on your life.

Not having a pet to talk to, hug tight, laugh at, play with, learn from, and shed tears over is far worse than never having had that relationship. Tough times in my life were eased having an animal companion at my side, and the good times were made even brighter. I can't imagine going through life any other way.

One thing I know for sure. I am who I am today because a special dog loved me—from the moment I entered her world.

HOLIDAY TRADITIONS

Two sets of eyes met that Thanksgiving, orchestrated by a higher purpose—a destiny moment that would change their lives and bless lives beyond them.

Calm in the center of the pack of rambunctious pups, one sat still, looking up at the lean, dark-haired man dressed in a burgundy flannel shirt, denim Wranglers, and brown polished cowboy boots. Drawn by her silent admiring gaze, Eddie lifted the four-month-old Pekingese/Dachshund puppy up onto the velvet sofa to cuddle. He placed her along the side of his thigh and let her nestle inside the den his weight made on the living room couch. The touch of his hand stroking her fawn-colored, silken hair lulled the puppy to sleep.

Agnes and Gianni hosted dinner at their home

in Merced, California every Thanksgiving since their marriage began in the 1950s. By 1962, their gathering had grown to include two sons and one daughter, Agnes' parents Rosa and Francisco, and her newlywed sister and brother-in-law, Lena and Eddie. This year, the family added five new puppies to their household. One had already stolen Eddie's heart.

With Agnes being of Portuguese descent, and Gianni of Italian, it was not unusual to find Portuguese sweet bread in the same breadbasket as dinner rolls and an oblong bowl of raviolis situated by the turkey and stuffing. Green beans sautéed in olive oil and sweet potato casserole topped with mini-marshmallows created a unique European-American aroma. Whole cranberry sauce and an appetizer plate with a cheese ball in the center encircled by black and green olives, carrot slices, and party crackers, added to the festive spread. Gianni's favorite post-dinner football-watching snack—candy-coated walnuts made by Agnes—were of cinnamon-sugary bliss, so addictive to his guests that Gianni would stash a few for himself to enjoy later.

The slender brunette dressed in a ginger loose-fitting blouse which covered her third-trimester baby bump, a matching plaid skirt, and black ballerina flats, stood next to her sister at the threshold of the living and dining rooms. Agnes and Lena had finished preparing food in the kitchen and had laid everything across the autumn-designed table runner.

Agnes announced that the meal was ready in both English and Portuguese, her parents' native language. "*A comida está pronta,*" she said while motioning for Francisco and Rosa to come to the dinner table. Pointing to two dining chairs she had designated for them, one at the head of the table and the other next to it along the side, Agnes said, "*Mãe e Pai, sinta aqui.*"

Gianni's seven-year-old daughter stood up from playing with the puppies and ran to the dinner table declaring, "I've named the puppy next to Uncle Eddie. Her name is *Susie!*"

Lena smiled at her husband on the couch. Eddie lowered the drowsing pup into the huddle of four small canines on the hardwood floor below. "We'll be right back, Susie," Lena promised the precious curly-tailed darling with a cute little nose wrinkle between her short muzzle and deep brown eyes. The newlyweds agreed they would return after dinner and decide if she was "the one."

Susie looked on as kids and adults seated themselves at the holiday-decorated table, said grace, passed bowls and plates of food around, and then gobbled like it was their last meal. Susie's expression said *what was there really left to decide?* Instincts told her the decision had already been made. There was no choosing. She was theirs, created for a reason—her purpose planned.

Susie snuggled with her fur siblings while she waited for the couple to return, sensing a new home awaited her. The newlyweds hadn't planned to adopt a pet within two months of Lena's due date. Raising a puppy with a newborn child wouldn't even be on the list of things to do for most first-time parents, but they loved animals and knew the joy and companionship pets give to all ages. As strong Catholics, they believed in divine timing; meeting Susie was no coincidence.

Over dinner, Lena and Eddie recognized the Thanksgiving blessing before them. Susie was meant to be in their lives from that exact moment for the little person with no siblings who was soon to join their family. It was that simple.

SILVER BRANCHES

Hello, I am that little person. My parents named me Denise, and this is my story of the best dog and gift of life ever – Susie.

We weren't much difference in height, less than a yard. The height gap shortened further when she stretched upward for affection, placing two gentle front paws on my thigh. Who could resist a doggie hug with those beautiful brown, angelic eyes looking at them? Not me. I loved it!

The yummy food, the tree-decorating tasks, and the gifts that eventually appeared under the tree left Susie and I giddy with joy every Christmas. Our family tradition included eating popcorn while stringing garland around silver branches, drinking hot cocoa, and choosing the best spots on the tinsel tree to hang peppermint candy canes, ornaments, and more tinsel.

The work always began in our small kitchen. Coils glowed on the electric burners of our white stove. Jiffy Pop duty was my welcomed assignment every Christmas tree-decorating afternoon. I held the attached handle with a white potholder, a red poinsettia stitched into its middle, crocheted by my grandmother Rosa (known as Ava to me, the Portuguese translation for grandmother.)

While Mom stood by, I gently shook the pan back and forth over the burner and pictured my Ava doing the same thing with me at her house on weekend visits. At Ava's house, we'd also bake cookies from scratch. I can still picture Ava opening the oven door, pulling a cookie sheet full of sugar cookies topped with holiday sprinkles out—steam fogging her gold-rimmed eyeglasses—setting the warm cookies down on a trivet on the counter, and "product testing" one before it cooled.

Mom heated instant cocoa mix with Borden's whole milk in a cooking pot on another burner until the aroma of sweet chocolate permeated the air. Then, she'd pour hot chocolate into mugs and pile whipped cream on top as high as I convinced her was required per Santa.

Kernels popped until they pushed the aluminum

foil into a round balloon. Mom would slit open my Jiffy Pop creation with a steak knife, and I'd empty the avalanche of corn into individual bowls. Susie sat on the linoleum floor, watching the event unfold, raising her shiny brown muzzle upward, her head bobbing in the air with nostrils moving, for a hint at what tasty morsel might be coming her way.

We moved to the living room where Bing Crosby and Perry Como 78-rpm vinyl records played Christmas music on the old RCA Victor. There, a sparse tinsel tree developed into a densely decorated silvery pine by our family of four, three humans dressed in red plaid flannel pajamas and a dog clad in her green, red, and white knit sweater.

Though we didn't outfit ourselves in hooded coats and winter gloves, drive miles to a Christmas tree farm, choose a fragrant, fresh Douglas fir, drag it to our car and strap it to the rooftop for the ride home, our family memories were no less special. The view from outside, for anyone peering through the bay window into our annual holiday workshop, would make even Norman Rockwell proud.

My parents had purchased an artificial tinsel Christmas tree from the Sears Catalog the first year they were married because of the alluring easy payment plan. It was their gift to each other and to the family they were starting. Owning an aluminum Christmas tree was economical, especially for a young family of farmers like mine who lived on a budget and didn't have spare money to buy real trees every year.

Christmas was extra special for Susie and me. On the first weekend after Thanksgiving, we'd follow Dad to my parents' bedroom closet where he'd pull a three-foot box from behind hanging clothes and bring it to our annual project location in the living room. Susie and I sat on the carpet observing while he pieced together the trunk until it rose to its six-foot height, placed it in a lightweight aluminum stand, and then wrapped it with a white, sequin fleece blanket.

Since Dad was the tallest family member, he had the task of crowning the tree's peak with our family's treasured keepsake, a red glass Santa tree topper. Spun of thin glass and adorned with red, silver, and white gems, handling the topper made us all nervous for fear of breaking it. It glistened with Santa's snowy beard curled for much of its length, draping down the treetop. The priceless decoration atop our tinsel tree captivated me.

Mom would remove individually wrapped branches from the cardboard box and categorize each of them according to their tiny, color-coded dots, spreading groups across the low pile carpeting.

After Susie sniffed approval of every silver branch with aluminum foil needles, I would match the color-coded dot at its tip to the same one on an eighth inch round opening in the aluminum tree trunk and insert. Obedient, Susie sat awaiting further instructions if I commanded them. Branches of different lengths required attention to detail to meet the triangular-shaped goal.

I was obsessed with putting jigsaw puzzles together as a kid. I spent hours on this task, kneeling on the floor at the coffee table with Susie on the couch behind me, analyzing the structure of each piece, and sometimes getting her approval before placing it on the board.

Hanging ornaments and garland on a Christmas tree is a cheery pastime many of us enjoy, but building an artificial tree one piece at a time for an avid puzzle-fan like me was way more fun. I recall my excitement the year I inserted branches higher up the tree trunk because I had grown taller than the previous Christmas. Susie looked up at me with her big brown eyes, wiggled and wagged her tail, and opened her mouth to where I was convinced, she was smiling at me. Though a dog technically wouldn't understand why

I was overjoyed, my connection with Susie was strong. If I was happy, Susie was happy and vice versa. Now, that's what I call true friendship.

I have vivid memories of helping my mother set up the electric color wheel, with four plastic parts of equal quarters, which sat on the floor next to the tree and shined rotating colors of green, red, orange, and blue hues upon it. I also remember how hot that machine got with prolonged use. That contraption was a fire waiting to happen!

My folks drilled into me we were never to leave the wheel running when we weren't in the house. Before we left home or went outside to do chores, Mom or Dad would say to me or each other, "Don't forget to unplug the wheel!" If we were already in the middle of feeding the farm animals or were in the car heading to town and for some reason the *reminder* hadn't occurred earlier, I'd hear those infamous words spoken to me or the other parent, "Did you unplug the wheel?"

I have vague memory of a time or two when chores were interrupted by this question, and a walk to the house or a return car ride home was made to ensure the wheel had been unplugged. Better to be safe than sorry!

On the rare occasion that we all forgot, and the wheel ran nonstop for an hour or two, I remember watching whoever entered the house first and realized it was still going 'round and 'round, run to unplug it. Maybe that's why fire has always been my biggest fear.

PRICELESS GIFTS

Susie had only one doggie knit sweater that she received as a Christmas gift one year. It was green, red, and white, Christmas colors, but it was her trademark look throughout winter. On Christmas day, she sat next to me by the tinsel tree in her holiday attire as I opened presents knowing her patient presence would eventually lead to personal bliss.

One of my earliest memories at Christmas, was the time I received a gift from my parents which symbolized my father's pride as a volunteer firefighter in our community. I was sitting on the floor with Susie beside me when I opened a present I couldn't figure out how to work. My dad got up from our tan, mid-century modern sofa and came to my rescue.

I sat baffled at how to operate the brick-red fire engine with its elongated white ladder. Dad knelt beside me and pointed out the features of my (and his) new toy. He turned the fire engine on. It lurched forward, sirens blaring, red lights flashing! I scrammed, with Susie trailing close behind, crying in fear for my life, never to return to the scene of the fire. At the age of four, I extinguished my future of following in my father's footsteps as a volunteer firefighter.

The next year, my parents gave me a plastic, battery-operated toy train set. Unwrapping that gift was a gentler, more delightful experience than the screaming fire engine. I spent hours on Christmas day playing with it, while Susie followed the train around the track. My dad later fastened the tracks to a sheet of plywood and attached a block and tackle locking system to the four corners so the plywood could be hung from the ceiling. That way, it saved floor space and we wouldn't have to re-assemble the tracks every time we wanted to play.

Until I was old enough to do it myself, Mom or Dad pulled the rope through the cables to lower the plywood from the ceiling to the floor. Boy was I a lucky girl to have them as parents!

My Ava hosted Christmas dinner for my aunts and uncles and cousins on my mother's side until my grandfather's failing health and subsequent passing. After that, we celebrated Christmas dinner at our home, and my grandmother spent all of Christmas day with us.

As the youngest grandchild, I loved spending time with my Ava. She treated me and Susie as sisters. When my family went to Ava's house for mid-morning or afternoon visits, she had us gather at her kitchen table for foods common in her homeland, the land of my ancestors.

One of our favorite snacks was Portuguese sweet bread with butter spread on it and cheddar cheese slices cut from a two-pound block. Ava would break off pieces of bread and cheese and hand them down to Susie sitting at her feet, looking up at her from the floor. I remember watching my grandmother, during my weekend stays at her house, churn her own butter, which by the way, turned out to be delicious! It's no wonder Susie stayed close to Ava. She followed her every move, salivating in anticipation of Ava's offerings.

After we opened our gifts on Christmas morning each year, I'd walk with Susie over to the red felt stocking that Mom made, inscribed with the name *Susie* in silver glitter, tacked above the colorful faux andirons and flickering flames of our Sears Catalog's red cardboard brick fireplace. I'd pull out a wrapped rectangular-shaped stocking-stuffer and show it to her at nose level. She'd smell it, nose twitching and tail wagging.

While I ripped off the outer gift wrap as quickly as kids do, Susie wiggled faster. The look of heavenly bliss on Susie's face brought smiles to all of us when she first saw the unveiled brown wrapper—a full-sized milk chocolate bar.

♦ ♦ ♦

Halloween was the only other holiday where Susie expected a milk chocolate treat. We'd both wear costumes out trick-or-treating. One year, I dressed up as Casper the Friendly Ghost, and Susie was Micky Mouse. Poor Susie. She was trying to be a good sport, but her mask kept sliding to the side.

Since I lived in the country and homes were acres apart, I was one of those kids whose parents drove them into town to go trick-or-treating. We'd start out at a close family friend's home. I was right in the middle of her two daughters in age. While we kids went door to door, our mothers followed, chaperoning from the sidewalk. My mom pulled my red Radio Flyer wagon with Susie seated inside, enjoying her unexpected nighttime ride.

When our treat bags were filled to the rim, we piled into our 1968 blue half-ton Dodge pickup and drove to my grandmother's home across town. Ava looked forward to our visit and seeing our costumes.

I'll never forget the first Halloween after my parents bought a new truck. We were traveling on curvy Bear Creek Drive, and "Pop!" What was that? "Pop! Pop! Pop!" The yellow gooey liquid covered our windshield in seconds, and we realized we were the target of an egg attack. The wipers helped clear the mess, but we were all shaken by the attack while the truck was moving on a narrow road along a creek. Those hoodlums could have killed us!

Even years later, my mom remembers that she glanced at the three of us kids seated between her and the other mom. Our jaws had dropped, and we were looking straight ahead—disbelief written all over our faces. Susie sat on my lap looking forward, too. The popping sounds sent her into protective mode, and she began to bark. Once the pelting stopped, her job was done. She relaxed and watched as the unfamiliar (to her) egg substance slid down the windshield.

Our moms chose not to stop—that it was safer to get to Ava's house first. When we arrived, they jumped out of the truck and quickly washed off all traces of egg yolk. Unfortunately, the impact left a white, egg-size imprint on the hood. We felt both empathy for the brand-new Dodge, with a now noticeable flaw, and anger toward the miscreants for causing the damage.

When peddling for treats had ended that Halloween night and we were back home, Susie rushed to my side as I emptied the candy bag on the living room carpet to revel in my bounty. She instantly spotted the full-sized milk chocolate bar Ava had given us. We sat together on the floor and watched each other savor our shared delectable gift.

Back in those days, we had no idea that chemicals and caffeine in chocolate could poison dogs. The revelation was something my family had not known back in the 1960s and 1970s. Not until my adulthood did I learn these terrifying facts. It's best to avoid giving dogs chocolate all together. Thank goodness Susie never became ill from her semi-annual treats.

Susie would stay at my grandmother's house when we went out of town to attend my father's Lather's Union conventions. As a building construction lath and plasterer finishing interior walls and ceilings, my dad had become secretary of his local union in the late 1960s. Dad did this in addition to being a farmer.

My grandmother enjoyed Susie's company since she spent so much time alone after becoming a widow. She enjoyed her company so much that she turned her home into a doggie nail salon. Ava recognized how much I liked watching my mother paint her nails, and she knew I'd miss Susie while we were gone. Ava wanted me to be even happier to see Susie when I got back home. She had an idea.

With bows attached to the short tan hair on her head, and her toenails painted shades of pink to bright red, our little country dog became citified. The first time we saw this transformation when we picked up Susie, Mom said to Ava, "Now I know why you asked for my bottles of fingernail polish!"

Ava understood and spoke English around me since my parents hadn't taught me Portuguese, but I connected with my roots when she spoke in her native language. Ava looked at me, then Susie, and then back at me, and said, "*Bonita.*"

Mom translated, "Pretty."

I said, "She is. My dog is so pretty, Ava!"

Susie strutted ahead of me to the door to go home, with an attitude like she was first up on the runway during New York's fashion week.

TRUE OBEDIENCE

As an only child, my adventurous ways sometimes landed me in hot water, well maybe not hot, but lukewarm for sure. One time, I set out to create a taller dog or to simply find out how far I could go. All I have is a fragmented memory of my devilish deed, but it does make me chuckle when I replay the events of that day and ask myself, *"What was I thinking?"*

Most little kids like playing with alphabet building blocks. I had a greater fondness because my father worked in construction. I wanted to build things like my daddy.

One afternoon, with an idea in my head and mom fixing dinner, I grabbed one of the folded metal TV trays leaning against our living room wall and took it to my bedroom, with Susie following close behind. The trays were used mostly on Friday nights for popcorn and soda pop (or whiskey highballs for the adults.)

I opened the tray and snapped each of the four corners into place. I laid down a dozen building blocks around the edges. Then I hoisted Susie atop. Being the obedient companion she was, Susie stood as ordered, attentive and awaiting further instruction. I began my experiment, picking up each paw and methodically placing one building block underneath until all four were equal.

I paused and took in my now inch-taller dog. *Ah, not enough.* I grabbed another building block, picked up one leg, added a block on top of the first row and set Susie's leg back down. As I was rounding the bend and adding a second block to the next foot, the TV tray began to wobble, escalating Susie's fear of the unknown as she rode out the rip currents.

Dad came into my room to say, "Dinner is ready!" He rushed to us, pulled Susie off the TV tray and onto solid ground below, and said, "Don't do that again." That was my first and last attempt to see what my little dog would look like as a tall Great Dane.

I don't recall my infatuation with commercials, but my parents tell me I would run into our living room from anywhere I was in earshot of the TV when one came on. I'd stand in front of our television, fully engrossed until the show resumed. It was one of those times that I lost sight of Susie; she wasn't beside me after the commercial break. I remember combing the house and yard, along with my mom and dad, searching for her. It was not like Susie to be away from me. We were perplexed. We cried out, "Susie!" and "Come here, Susie! Where are you, Susie?"

Next to my bedroom at the front of the house was a small room my dad used as an office with an architect drafting table for estimating building construction. My mom's Singer sewing machine (a high school graduation gift from her parents) and an unfolded ironing board stood in the opposite corner. A black antique upright piano squeezed in against the wall.

Susie and I would hang out with Mom when she was sewing or ironing clothes. I'd roll my doll buggy around the house and occasionally in the yard with some occupant inside. There might be a doll or two in the buggy, even our cat, Socks. But most of the time, Susie was the passenger.

After we failed to find Susie, we circled back, searching every room again. Stationed underneath the opened ironing board, precisely where I had parked it but had forgotten, sat my covered doll buggy. Normally, the white hard plastic cover was pulled open, revealing its contents. None of us had noticed its different appearance as we passed by earlier.

It had to be a mother's instinct to cause my mom to feel the pull of her fur child's energy and walk over to my doll buggy, pulling up the cover. There she was! Susie, all tucked in and staying put as she had been instructed to do by an easily distracted child.

I'd accompany my mom for afternoon chores around the ranch. One of her chores was tossing alfalfa hay into our Angus herd's manger, which wrapped halfway around the haystack. Mom instructed me and Susie to stand in an open area away from the haystack, a safe distance from hay flakes and hungry cows. I stood by and enjoyed a peanut butter and strawberry jelly sandwich, with Susie at my feet, waiting for me to share part of my snack with her. I was five at the time, when one horrifying day the chores didn't go as planned.

The pitchfork sat pierced into one hay bale resting five high atop the stack. It ordinarily loosened on demand. That day, it wedged in deeply. Mom wrestled trying to dislodge the pitchfork as the hay bale teetered over the edge. The wobbly hay bale tilted with each frantic struggle, eventually falling to the ground, with the pitchfork dislodged during the fall. Once the bale landed, the impact caused the pitchfork to skyrocket in my direction.

I was standing on the truck path naturally made over time by fallen pieces of hay about ten feet from the haystack, savoring my PB&J sandwich, when a flying pitchfork slid straight down my face. In shock, I grasped my face as blood flowed into my left hand. Mom screamed, racing to my aid with maternal terror in her voice.

Dad ran across the yard, yelling at Mom, "How could you let this happen?"

"It was an accident!" Mom answered through her tears. Susie paced back and forth, and I understood she was trying to figure out how she could help each one of us.

Dad picked me up as blood streamed down my face. He carried me from the scene, firing back, "You're a bad mother!" His frustration boiled over because he had warned her not to move large stacks of hay with a pitchfork due to instability.

"Daddy, don't be mean to Mommy! It's not her fault!" I yelled while in his arms.

Mom shouted, "It was an accident!" as she scooped up Susie and ran with Dad and me to the house.

The accident, and heated exchange between my

parents, and what I said in defense of my mother, revealed integrity and a resilience beyond my years. The advocacy I showed for those in distress makes me proud, knowing I always had it in me. Whenever I think about being hit by a pitchfork, my body is transported back into those little five-year-old's courageous shoes. Trauma isn't something one forgets.

When we made it to the house, Mom put Susie on the couch in the living room while Dad grabbed the car keys. We leaped into the family car and rushed off to the emergency room. I sat on the black and white checkered vinyl bench seat of our silver 1960 Chevrolet Impala in the middle of my parents, with Mom pressing a washcloth to the side of my face as dad drove. Both remained at odds with one another.

The hospital patched me up and sent us home within a few hours. Since the pitchfork hit my face on the left side of my mouth, my emergency room pediatrician didn't want to use stitches. Instead, he applied cocoa butter on my skin and used surgical tape to cover the holes from each puncture.

When we entered our driveway, we saw Susie sitting on the top cushion of the back of the couch, looking out the window, appearing worried. I can imagine how she must have felt from the fear in our voices and speeding away, leaving her behind with only the company of a cat.

When I walked in the front door of our house, Susie looked at the white surgical tape on half of my face and approached slowly. She'd normally be excited to greet us, especially who we thought she considered to be her sister. But that day, she understood it was important to be careful around an injured person. I went to our couch, pulled my legs up onto it and laid down on my back, my head on the throw pillow. Susie hopped up beside me and laid on her stomach, her head lowered in between her front legs, eyes saddened as she looked up at me.

It's okay, Susie. You don't have to worry anymore. I'm fine now. That's because you're here with me.

DANCE PARTNERS

I loved playing 45-rpm vinyl records on my children's record player. My favorites were "Denise" by Randy and The Rainbows and "My Girl" by the Temptations, and I played them over and over again. I'd sing along word for word and dance to the music. As an adult, I learned a startling fact about my namesake song "Denise"—the two lyrics used often in the song were "dooby doo" and not *Scooby Doo*. I often sang and danced with my dog, and was a fan of the cartoon *Scooby Doo*, so to me, the vocalist on the record HAD to be saying *Scooby Doo* instead.

I loved "My Girl" because my daddy told me he cherished the song as it made him think of me, since it came out when I was a toddler. All my life, I have felt special in his eyes because of that song's lyrics. I'm grateful for that eternal connection with my father.

When I danced to "My Girl" with Susie, I believed it was written for *my* girl, the dog I adored, who was my sunshine.

My dance partner was always ready and willing for fun adventures with me. *Susie, wanna dance?* When those brown eyes sparkled and a smile appeared on her face, I grabbed some dancing clothes and put them on her. She'd have to stand on her hind legs, front paws in my hands, and swing back and forth. If we danced in the morning, I'd be wearing pajamas, and she'd be cloaked in my child's bathrobe with a knit head scarf tied under her neck. You could barely see her adorable face peeking through all that garb or her back paws covered by the robe. My goodness, what that poor dog had to endure.

When I was in first grade, I contracted a viral infection. I can still picture the embarrassing day in my classroom. My teacher hurried me to the principal's office to call home as I left a trail of vomit behind. My parents rushed to school to pick me up and take me to my pediatrician. The doctor examined me and sent me home with medication and a recommendation to drink plenty of liquids and rest.

But that bug was not done with me. I became increasingly weaker and dehydrated. My condition deteriorated so rapidly that I was rushed to the emergency room and immediately admitted to Mercy Hospital. Doctors told my parents if they had arrived just two hours later, it would have been too late.

At that time, the Dominican Sisters of Kenosha, Wisconsin managed Mercy Hospital. I remember friendly nuns smiling at me, praying hands in position, as they entered my room. I'm guessing they understood how sick I was. The extremely sick little girl needed healing prayers.

My hospitalization lasted five days. A nurse set up a cot next to my bed so I'd have a parent with me during the night. My parents rotated shifts to keep me company. I'd be excited when they'd bring a new coloring book, game, or children's picture book. I loved having at least one parent with me at all times. It definitely helped me get well. But one family member was missing—Susie.

The hospital didn't allow pets. I would have recovered faster if Susie could have slept with me in my bed. Whenever I was sick at home, resting on the couch or in bed, Susie was by my side. My canine nurse had healing powers no one else could match. This was something hospitals didn't understand at the time.

After my five-day stay, the hospital discharged me

and sent me home. It felt like forever being away from Susie. I couldn't wait to see my buddy and hug her tight.

On the way out of the hospital, Mom said, "Susie hasn't been the same since you left. I find her body slumped on the floor with her neck flat inside her outstretched front legs, eyes discouraged, and sometimes watery." She shook her head.

The car's tires crunched the gravel driveway as we arrived home and stopped at the door of our house. Susie sat on the blue and white crochet afghan on top of the sofa, that my grandmother had knitted to preserve the life of the sofa, peeking out the front window. When Mom and I got out of the car, she barked loudly.

Mom unlocked the door and opened it for me to enter first. My little Pekinese/Dachshund tornado whirled through the opening, whining and circling us at roadrunner speed, ears and tongue flapping in the wind. She finally stopped, crouched down, looked at us, and planned her next move. Then, she jumped up to my stomach and slid down my front legs.

I bent over to grab her body, but she jumped again. This time, I was off balance, and we both collapsed onto the floor. I laid back, smiling and giggling as Susie feverishly licked my face, squirming as I hugged and stroked her fawn-colored hair that I had so missed. She planted the much-needed doggie kisses all over my face.

My fur sister, my loyal companion, my partner in crime, and my dance partner was at my side—we were united once again. It was the best moment of my life, and if Susie could talk, I think she would have said the same.

MIGHTY PROTECTOR

Susie had this habit of barking and running full speed up the sofa and onto the top of the backrest every time something outside came into view which she thought threatened her family. One time she was going so fast she overshot the top of the couch and fell down the narrow gap between it and the wall. She came right out from behind the couch, shook off the error (literally), and carried on.

There was no such thing as an underground cable where we lived. Wooden poles held black, thick power lines extending far into the horizon along the other side of the country road. One set of wires crossing the road to a solitary power pole at our ranch provided us with electricity. Those lines would wave in the wind after a high profile vehicle whisked by at top speed.

Typically, in summer, eighteen-wheelers would take

back roads where there was less traffic to move historic homes from one location to another. I remember as a kid running to our living room window when we'd see the rigs approaching. It became quite an exciting event to witness how the movers handled the challenge presented to them.

I'd kneel on the sofa and lean my upper body against the backrest, with Susie on the top cushion, peering through the window and watching the front lead truck pull to the side of the road, followed by a worker jumping out. Amber lights flashed above a draped sign across the truck that read "WIDE LOAD." The driver traveling behind in a pickup with glaring caution lights would pull over to the side of the road.

Two burly guys in short-sleeved shirts with orange reflective vests and work boots vaulted to the top of the old house on the flatbed truck. Using sticks, they held the dangling electric lines up as the semi crept underneath. Sometimes my parents would join Susie and me at the window. We'd hold our breath as the operation ensued, hoping we wouldn't lose all power. We cheered when the life-threatening feat was accomplished, relieved that the lights would stay on, and the well would keep pumping water.

A neighbor who lived behind our ranch, a country

mile away, would ride her horse along the road and into another farmer's property on the weekend. I don't remember her ever walking her horse; she always trotted or galloped with her two dogs running off-leash. Perhaps her horse had pent-up energy from not being ridden much during the week, or it was young with natural high energy. Or maybe she was running away from her six kids, even if just for an afternoon.

Every time Susie would notice the horse and dog trio speeding by, she'd run through our house and up the sofa to the window barking in annoyance to issue a fierce warning. Her small-dog protective quality was endearing when it occurred indoors. One summer afternoon, however, Susie found herself in an unexpected situation.

Mom was pruning and watering rosebushes with a garden hose while I ate chocolate chip cookies and lounged on the front lawn with Susie. Our neighbor was traveling on horseback on the dirt shoulder of the paved road. Her two large dogs ran alongside. Susie started barking and ran toward the crew in full-on protection mode. She trusted that she was safe within her own property lines.

Hearing Susie's bark, the largest of the two German Shepherds stopped. He turned and glared at Susie.

Our peaceful summer day suddenly burst like a balloon. The German Shepherd charged toward Susie, growling, teeth bared, lips curled, and hair on his back standing on end.

Mom shouted, "Stop! Get back! Go away!" and chased after Susie.

I trailed behind and yelled, "Get Away!" Like the canine attacker was going to listen to me and my childish voice.

Mom hurried to get ahead of Susie, but the German Shepherd beat us to her. He clenched his teeth into Susie's neck. He shook her body like a wild animal clutching and trying to kill its prey. Susie let out a primal yelp. Mom forced the dogs apart enough to pull Susie to safety. Blood gushed from Susie's neck; one leg went limp.

By then, our neighbor had caught up, dismounted her horse, and grabbed her dangerous dog. She said, "I'm sorry."

But neither my mom nor I had it in us to accept her apology. We were still in shock…and mad. *Your dog hurt our Susie!* The poor girl was minding her own business on her property, and this off-leash dog viciously attacked her. Sorry neighbor. It's gonna take us a while to forgive your dog for hurting our family member.

Mom put Susie in the cab of our pickup, while I jumped in, and she retrieved her purse and keys from the house. My mother remained a strong leader throughout the ordeal. I tried to mimic her strength, but tears rolled down my face. *Susie, my sweet girl. It isn't fair! You were just protecting us. Why, oh why?*

Mom raced to the veterinary clinic where they treated Susie for her injuries. Luckily, the German Shepherd didn't bite Susie deep enough to cause internal injuries. She could have been killed if he had grabbed Susie in a different manner. I suppose the scruff of her neck was thick enough to protect her from a worse outcome. Susie's sore leg must have been a by-product of the struggle. The veterinarian stitched her up and sent her back home to rest.

Pekingese and Dachshunds are known to be loyal family companions and good watchdogs, and Dachshunds especially may take on animals much larger than themselves. Susie's mix of both breeds explained her courageous instincts to run after the German Shepherd. After a few days convalescing, Susie was back on duty, playing with me outside and ready to defend her people and property like usual.

SWEET DREAMS

I think every kid should grow up in an old farmhouse. The life experience it provides is unmatched. When you become an adult and live in a new house in the suburbs, you wonder how you even survived a childhood without modern conveniences. That upbringing reminds you of where you came from and keeps you grounded in all you do. I feel blessed to have grown up in a one-hundred-year-old house. It has always motivated me to strive for more; and yet, I already had everything I needed…unconditional love.

Pale blue aluminum siding surrounded our home, having been added after an addition was built to the back half by the previous owner. As the years rolled by, the hardwood floorboards in our home became spongy to walk on, making us wonder if they might not spring back up some day. The kitchen's black and white checkered linoleum flooring had an obvious slant upward from the back door. The harder it poured during heavy winter storms, the more cooking pots we pulled out of the white cupboard and spread around the kitchen floor to catch water falling from the ceiling. The slant of the bathroom floor caused us to pray it held for the duration of our visits.

It was a bit common in those old homes to have rodent problems. When we were sitting in the living room watching television after dinner, wood-gnawing sounds inside the wall overshadowed characters speaking on the screen. Sometimes, we'd even hear rats scamper to and fro. Although we weren't fond of those hungry little critters, we couldn't help but laugh at our unusual reality.

I don't remember hearing *crunch, crunch, crunch* in the daylight hours, but that could have been because I was engrossed in Mom's storytelling. Every afternoon, from the age of two until third grade (when Mom started working as a teacher's aide at my grammar school) she'd read at least two children's books a day to me and Susie. She had me pick each book from my personal library before we sat on the couch. It's where my love for books began, and my imagination soared, with Mom and my bestie at my side.

We didn't have central heating and air. Our air conditioning was either an open window or a fan. I loved it when my mom moved the water cooler fan from the living room to my bedroom. It lulled me to sleep on sweltering summer nights with its mist and humming, almost enough to block out the wood-munching sounds.

I wasn't scared at all with Susie sleeping next to me in my bed. She loved me and would always be there for me. With my protector in place, I could fall into dreamland and not worry. My miniature guard dog would fight any rat that escaped the wall and attacked me.

Saturday mornings when I didn't have to rush off to school, Susie and I had time to relax. Donning a red fleece with white trim bathrobe, I'd drag my kid-size wooden rocker from the sidelines to be directly in front of our mahogany RCA console TV. Then I'd pull Susie into my lap and become enthralled by *The Flintstones* and *The Jetsons* cartoons. I don't know how Susie did it, laying on her back in my lap while I cartoon binge-watched. Maybe she was too tired to move after guarding me from gigantic rats all night.

SQUIRREL VS. CANINE

A couple of years after my parents bought their pickup truck for the ranch, they won a prize at the county fair. It was a white camper which fit perfectly onto the truck bed—not a millimeter bigger or smaller. There's no question it had to be divinely sent to fit that good.

As a volunteer firefighter in our community, my father became good friends with volunteer fire chief Sammy. When Sammy learned we had won a camper (word traveled fast through the fire station), he invited us to join his family for the weekend at Fish Camp, a tiny Mariposa County town just outside the South entrance to Yosemite National Park.

I looked forward to being in nature in a new area, and I had no doubt Susie would love sniffing an abundance of mountain smells and exploring the land with me.

Sammy led the way driving his truck in front of us into the park, explaining to the forest ranger at the entry gate that we were with him. We meandered through the narrow paved road already lined with camping equipment, vacationers, truck bed campers, and staked tents. Pine scents infused our noses and fresher air entered our lungs through the open windows as we journeyed to our campsite. Susie's ecstatic upper body hung over the passenger door, her legs anchored in Mom's lap, tongue hanging out, nose flared, and ears flapping in the wind.

Dad pulled into our campsite adjoining Sammy's and turned off the truck. Mom pulled Susie's entire body into the cab and said, "We're here!"

I seconded that with long-awaited excitement. "We're finally here!"

Next Mom announced, "Pee pee time!" After a long drive on winding roads through the mountains, Mom didn't just mean that for Susie.

At home on the ranch, Susie didn't need a leash. We lived on twenty acres, and mostly farm equipment traveled the country road next to our ranch. Susie knew the property line and never ventured past it.

SQUIRREL VS. CANINE

Fish Camp sat in the mountains among redwoods where wildlife roamed free. Critter scents amid the evergreens easily beckoned a canine newcomer, especially one with Dachshund blood flowing through her veins. Dachshunds were bred in Germany hundreds of years ago to hunt badgers, which their name reflects. *Dach* translates to badger, and *hund* means dog.

When Mom opened the passenger door, Susie bolted out quicker than a Greyhound through the entrance to a dog's wonderland. Our Dachshund had caught sight of a silver-gray squirrel. The instinctual hunt was on!

She barreled down the road, jumping over obstacles in her way, in pursuit of that fuzzy, long-bodied rodent. Mom yelled, "Susie! Susie!" All of us ran after Susie, Mom and I repeatedly calling her by name. We worried a passing car would hit her, or she would get lost in the forest. We hurried in the direction she fled.

Who knows how the squirrel outsmarted its predator, but it got away. Susie stopped her pursuit of her bushy-tailed target when she lost sight of it and heard us calling her name. She retreated back toward our group with an arrogance suggesting what she did was all in a day's work and wasn't her fault. Mom warned her: "Don't you dare do that again!"

All I cared about was picking Susie up and embracing her. I whispered in her velvety ear, "Oh, Susie, I'm so glad you came back. I don't know what I would have done if you got lost. It would have broken my heart!"

Susie turned her head back to me, licked my face, and wiggled her way out of my arms and onto the ground. She moved forward, sniffing the terrain, ready for her next adventure in the woods…on a leash.

BICYCLING BUDDIES

Before I learned how to ride a bike, I'd sit behind my mother on the banana seat of her cruiser bicycle. Susie sat in a plastic basket attached to the butterfly handlebars adorned with pink, yellow, and blue flowers. All three of us would travel the country roads within a five-mile radius from home.

How peaceful it was to feel a gentle breeze blow past us as we enjoyed our ride, absorbing the sights and sounds of livestock grazing and tractors plowing, and whiffs of fresh-cut alfalfa.

When I turned six and began riding my Schwinn with training wheels, my dad had to find a way for Susie to be with me since my dog-sister and I were inseparable. My handy dad built a rectangular wooden box just big enough for Susie to sit in comfortably and attached it to the back of my bicycle.

Susie sat behind me in the wooden box painted black, taking in the scenery to the left and right, as we rode the circular gravel driveway on our property. I was not allowed to ride on the paved road without a parent. We'd happily go round and round, and the repetition of our travels on the driveway often sparked my pet duck's curiosity.

Duckie, the oh, so creative name that I had christened him, would start off trailing behind us as I peddled my bicycle. His orange legs would move faster and faster with his webbed feet pounding the ground, as his waddling body tried to shorten the gap. Duckie didn't like being left behind. If the gap widened beyond his liking, he'd take a shortcut across the driveway to stand in front of us. He'd quack once there, reminding me to stop and pet his creamy white plumage before I did anything else.

Susie's bicycle voyages weren't trouble-free though. When I grew old enough to have the training wheels removed, there were days when I had a tough time staying upright. If I turned too sharp and lost my balance, guess what that meant for the bike, Susie, and me? Luckily, Susie was young enough to leap to safety. Me, not so much. My knees and elbows succumbed to more than one bloody scrape. But my canine nurse always came to my rescue and licked my wounds when I hit the gravel.

Besides bicycling, Susie and I enjoyed kiddie pool "swimming" and ice cream cones in summer. My parents purchased a 10-inch-high round, inflatable kiddie pool. Susie and I supervised Mom inflating the pool with a car tire air pump each summer.

The extreme heat was hard on chubby Susie. I didn't like seeing her pant fast and become sluggish while outdoors waiting for the portable pool installation to be complete. Once we filled the water to the rim, we jumped in and cooled off for the afternoon in the often triple-digit heat of the San Joaquin Valley. Susie stayed in the pool with me for hours, neither one of us in a hurry to get out. I enjoyed the scent of her damp hair while we waded. Any time I encounter wet-dog smell today, it pleasantly transports me back to swimming with my best friend.

Our day of cycling and pool time wasn't complete without mom fixing us a double scoop of vanilla ice cream on a cone. Mom made our treat, while Susie sat by me drooling.

Me and my girl would find a spot on the floor in front of our living room television and sit, Susie's eyes fixed on me with future expectation. A *Lassie* episode kept us company. Susie liked it best when I'd lay down on the carpet on my stomach, facing her at kid-to-dog eye level, with my double-scoop cake cone in hand.

I'd start by savoring a scrumptious lick from the bottom scoop to the top and then outstretch my frozen dairy dessert toward Susie. She accepted my offer without hesitation. One lick for me; one lick for Susie. That's how we rolled; two pals capping off a summer afternoon with the sweetest of summer delights.

PINE CASTLE

Living on a cattle ranch entailed working long hours. Whatever job my parents needed to do with the bulls, cows, and calves in the corral or pasture, they had to ensure their child was safe.

I was a fortunate girl to have a dad who built things for me. One of his many projects was a box structure, made of pinewood, mounted to the top of the corrals by the barn. It was situated at the edge of the wire fence by the paved road, high enough to where I felt like *queen of my castle* looking down upon the *commoners* below. I'd wave at neighbors traveling by in their cars, or I'd oversee my parents feeding and working cattle in the corrals.

I envied kids who had treehouses in their backyards, until I had something better. I wasn't stuck in a tree; I had land as far as I could see that sparked my imagination. My tree house (it could vouch for that since it was made of wood which comes from trees), had a wooden bench seat and a ladder that I climbed to get inside. My parents had to give me and Susie a lift until I was big enough to lift Susie up into it myself. I read books and shared snacks with Susie. It was our private retreat, where we occasionally invited guests over. But we liked it better when we were the only dwellers.

My parents bought Holstein calves from the auction yard to grow their cattle herd. It's typical for dairies to separate calves from their mothers soon after birth. Cows produce milk for about ten months after giving birth. Then they rest before they produce their next calf.

My parents would bottle-feed the calves in the corrals below my castle. One brown and white male bull calf was exceptionally gentle and loved to be petted. Susie and I would come down from our perch and step into the corrals to visit Brownie, my original name for him since he wasn't the typical black and white Holstein.

Impressionable at the age of six, I wanted to show the adult ranchers I was a true country girl. I could do my part and milk a cow (or a bull calf, I didn't know the difference) if necessary. I walked into the corral, pulled up a tin bucket, flipped it over, sat on the inverted bottom, put another bucket under Brownie's belly, and peered under him. Then, I made a fist with both hands and held them about six inches below Brownie's stomach, directly above the bucket. I squeezed my left hand, then my right hand, back to my left, and then back to my right, and so on and so on. One at a time… in the air.

My parents paused from their chores to watch me, curious as to what in the world I was doing. Susie stood next to me on the dirt mixed with dried manure on the ground. When I sensed I was being watched, I looked over at my parents.

Dad asked, "Did you have any luck milking Brownie?"

I said, "Yep."

Mom asked, "How much did you get?" *The moment of truth. Do I answer honestly, or do I prove that I'm just as good at milking as they are?*

I looked over at Susie, her head tilted, alert, facing my direction. Our eyes met; my thoughts connected with hers. For some reason it reminded me of one of our favorite TV shows at the time, *I Love Lucy*. *Okay, Ethel, you go along with me on this now, and the next time you chase a squirrel, Lucy's got your back.*

I answered, "A little bit." My parents laughed so hard, the neighbors a country mile away probably heard them. Susie ran over to my mom and barked. I wonder what she said to her.

✦ ✦ ✦

IN THE EARLY YEARS before our pole haybarn was built, our alfalfa haystack was located along the paved county road about four feet from the corrals. It was the only spot on our ranch where, if we needed to load hay onto the truck, we wouldn't get stuck in the mud after heavy storms.

One summer day, Mom and I were in the kitchen making sandwiches for lunch. Dad was watching TV in the living room. A loud vehicle coming down the road caught his attention, because he heard it slowing down at the beginning of our property, almost stopping at the entrance to our driveway. He got up from the couch and looked out the window, thinking we had a visitor. Instead, a green truck revved up and sped away. Dad explained to me, all these years later, that he "had a bad feeling."

As a volunteer firefighter, my dad was aware of a series of arsons happening in rural areas around the county. The odd behavior of that green truck didn't seem right.

He ran out the door and down the road. Mom, concerned by the commotion, set the bologna sandwich fixings down and rushed through the door. I flung a bag of potato chips on the counter and followed behind her, Susie at my heels.

We lost sight of Dad after he turned the corner by the milking barn. When we caught up to him, he was stomping out an ignited red traffic flare. It had landed in short weeds outside the fence, more than likely having ricocheted off the barbed wire fence. Mom grabbed a bucket and filled it with water from the spigot by the barn and poured it on the flare. It worked. Dad picked up the flare's end and threw it into Mom's empty bucket. Susie and I stood by each other horrified by what we witnessed and what could have happened.

Angels watched over us that day. My parents could have lost thousands of dollars in hay, wooden corrals, and the milking barn. It would have been devastating to my parents' cattle business and my family's livelihood. And most upsetting to Susie and me, our pine castle kingdom could have burned to the ground.

GETAWAYS & RISK-TAKERS

In the early 1970s, my parents purchased hill property near Lake McSwain in Mariposa County for the cattle to graze on from late fall to early spring. I, a pre-teen, and Susie, a middle-aged canine, looked forward to weekends there.

My parents took the white camper prize and removed it from the bed of our truck. They set the camper on top of the highest hill with the best views where it became our new memory-making getaway. They purchased a used white with red trim camping trailer and hauled it up there, too. Dad added plywood walls and a ceiling between both structures as a corridor to block out the cold and provide a short walkway between the truck camper door and the camping trailer.

If the weather permitted, we sat on various-sized,

moss-speckled granite boulders breaking through the Earth and ate our meals. The small, attached table in the camping trailer was nice, but it didn't have the same pizzazz as eating outdoors, overlooking the valley below and spotting wildlife in their habitat.

Nighttime on the hill proved incredible, away from city lights and obstructions. Stars sparkled in the dark sky. Mom used to say, "The stars are so close, I feel like I can reach out and touch them."

I enjoyed hearing packs of coyotes yipping and whistling in the night air, especially when a young one joined the choir. I wouldn't want to meet a coyote face to face, but it was so cute to hear a little one chime in with its higher-pitched youngster sound, trying to howl like the best of them.

Back in those days, walkie-talkies were big. They were black, hand-held, portable, two-way radio transceivers my parents used to communicate with me while Susie and I explored the hills. Walkie-talkies were fun to talk on, but I think because we were so far off the beaten path, the radio frequency range was limited. Our property was several miles from the paved road and nearest towns, and our transmitting reception was bad.

While my parents worked cattle or built fences,

Susie and I went on missions of geographical discovery. The land intrigued me, and I loved inspecting rocks, following a dirt cattle trail to find where it might lead, and pausing to observe a natural stream or pond.

Those walkie-talkies provided a false sense of security. If you asked my parents today, they would agree they should have kept a better eye on us. Both shared with me that at the time, when they were new Sierra Nevada foothill property owners, they didn't realize the potential hazards Susie and I could have encountered. From rattlesnakes to wild boars to tarantulas, God only knows what could have happened. We were lucky enough to occasionally spot a herd of deer, and that made our expedition worth the risk.

My parents slept in the camping trailer, and Susie and I had the main camper to ourselves, except for the time my Ava came to visit. Then it was a fun slumber party among us girls. We played games and ate snacks. And it was the first time my Ava wore pants!

Ava was born in 1902 on the island of Terceira, Azores. Portuguese custom expected women to wear only dresses, and Ava never freed that expectation since immigrating to the United States in 1921. Before our trip to the hill property that weekend, Mom had suggested Ava wear pants.

"The land is too rugged for dresses," Mom said. It would be a bold move if Ava consented.

When we arrived at Ava's house the morning of our trip, Ava opened the door and there, before our eyes, stood our cowgirl. She wore black trousers, my late grandfather's, a button-down shirt, cardigan, and closed toe leather shoes. Ava glowed, liberated in her western-ish duds, like a kid who finally got to do something she wasn't supposed to. She said, "*Vamos!*" and bounced into our truck, eager to hit the trail, smiling the whole while.

I have fond memories of all the times my Ava's daredevil ways emerged. Our country road was quiet when I was growing up. But when it was time for my Ava to go home after visiting us, look out! I'd yell, "Come on, Ava! Come on!" as she was about to leave the driveway.

Competitive seriousness covered her face as her eyes looked straight ahead, determining whether the road was clear. She'd punch the gas. Tire wheels spun in the gravel. She'd wave her left hand while not taking her eyes off the road, with Susie and me running along the fence by the road on our front lawn.

At the end of the fence line, I'd collapse onto my back under the Modesto Ash tree, breathing hard and laughing. Susie, panting from our sprint, would stop, lick salty tears off my face, and then roll over on the grass as if she were laughing herself. She'd pause on her back. I'd scratch her belly, and then she'd roll some more. I don't know why we were so inclined to race my grandmother, but we did.

RISE ABOVE

From the ages of eleven to thirteen, I was chubby. Kids at school had unkind things to say about my excess weight, but Susie's love for me never waned. After school, I'd gather sweet and fattening foods from our kitchen as soon as I got home and head to our living room. There, Susie would follow me to the coffee table where I spread my snack collection on top, slip in between it and our sofa, stretch my legs underneath the coffee table and lose myself in the fictional stories of *The Brady Bunch* and *Gilligan's Island* on our TV.

Susie sat to my right, looking up at me expecting an offer to share in my forget-the-mean-words-of-the-day indulgence. It's as if Susie understood what the bullies saw—an overweight and pimpled pre-teen with braces—was only my exterior. I was so much more. I loved books, wrote stories about ranch life, played musical instruments, showed horses, raised rabbits, and had been a Girl Scout and 4-H club member, to name a few of my accomplishments. But none of the bullies cared to find out those things about me because they didn't move beyond their first judgments.

"Three mean girls laughed at me today, Susie. They didn't have to say anything. I knew they were judging and talking about me by the way they giggled and stared at me from their silly huddle."

I could always count on Susie for whatever it was I was going through, and she'd be my biggest fan, partner in crime, sounding board, and a soft place to hide my tears. She'd be by my side because she loved me for who I was, not for what I looked like. She had proven it to me for as long as I could remember. In my eyes, Susie was the most beautiful dog in the world, and I believed that's how she saw me, except in human form.

"You've been around a long time, Susie, and you know me. YOU never judge me. You love me for the person I am on the inside. The brown hair on your nose has turned gray, but it doesn't change my feelings for you. You're the same sweet dog on the inside that I've always known and loved.

They're jealous of me, and I'm not going to let them

get me down! I will stand tall and be friendly even if they are not nice to me. I will focus on my schoolwork and getting good grades. With you, Susie, I know I can rise above any obstacle!"

After snack time, we'd often venture into the pasture to be around the horses. A foal born in 1976, named Freedom, was intrigued by our visit. He'd greet us each time, stretching his neck forward to me and then down to Susie's level, his nostrils sniffing us both in welcome. I'd stroke the velvety brown hair on Freedom's head, neck, and body while Susie would wander and inspect the surrounding area, muzzle to the ground.

It was obvious that the hands of time had slowed Susie's body down. Arthritis must have crept into her joints. She still enjoyed roaming the pasture, but she didn't go as far as she used to and would rest more often.

One day, I had a heart-to-heart talk with Freedom while Susie was exploring. "Freedom, Susie's getting old. She's my best friend. When she's gone, it'll be a sad, sad day. I feel a connection with you, too, ever since you were three days old. Will you be my new best friend when Susie goes to Heaven?" Freedom shoved me with his head, pushing me off balance for a second, and then he lowered his head and munched on grass.

I took his gesture as confirmation, like he was saying, "Don't worry. I got you girl!"

I found a nearby clover patch in the field and sat cross-legged. Susie returned as soon as she spotted me sitting on the ground at her level. Whenever I had extra time, I would sit and search for four-leaf clovers around our house or in the pasture. Ever since my mother found a four-leaf clover growing in our lawn, I was determined to find one for myself.

I remember that day. Mom jumped with joy! She carefully pulled it out of the ground and placed it in between the folds of a paper napkin and slipped it into an old book. We watched the lucky charm evolve over time into a pressed keepsake. No matter what unlucky situations arose, it reminded all of us that, as a family, we would get through anything.

CHRISTMAS SPIRIT

Mom was picking tomatoes and bell peppers from her vegetable garden. Dad, with a shovel resting on his right shoulder, was heading back to the field to tend to the irrigation. I was playing volleyball by myself, watching it land on top of the roof while waiting for the ball to roll back down so I could spike it back up, something I did regularly and thoroughly enjoyed. Susie was quiet, lying on her belly on the lawn, watching her family's activities.

It was a summer afternoon on the ranch. A day that should have gone with ease and predictability; instead, it was one of the worse days of my life.

Something told me to check on Susie. As I did, I saw her try to stand, then collapse on her side. All four legs were extended, and her whole body was rigid. Her head arched back, and her eyes rolled into their sockets. It took my breath away. "Susie, Susie!" I yelled as I ran to her.

I called my mom to come over. Dad heard us and rushed to Susie's side. We all tried to soothe Susie by speaking softly to her and stroking her hair. She was having a seizure, and it was horrible to witness. It must have been painful, and I couldn't stand seeing her in that state. She had a small seizure in the days leading up to this one, but it was over quickly. We never dreamed it could recur and become this powerful.

Then, stillness. Her body stopped moving. That was it.

When I realized Susie had exhaled for the last time, tears poured from my eyes. I didn't want to accept her death. "Su-sie. Don-'t l-ea-ve me," I managed to express between the tears, inhaling and exhaling each letter or syllable from my shattered heart.

We sat there around Susie, Dad saying, "Susie, old girl. You were the best dog a family could have."

Mom, unable to say much through her own tears, said, "Oh, Susie. I wish this weren't so."

I agreed. "Me, too, Susie. I wish you didn't have to leave. You were the best sister ever. My life will never be the same."

Mom said, "It's okay to let Susie go. Why don't you go inside."

Being farmers, we were used to animals being put down. This was different. Mom and Dad wanted to protect my feelings. They knew that watching the burial of my best friend would destroy me. They wanted to spare their teenage daughter additional heartache from the grim final memory of Susie being wrapped in towels, placed in a cardboard box, and buried below our towering Modesto Ash.

Her final resting place would be under the same tree where Susie and I rolled on the grass together, laughing as Ava sped away in her Ford four-door sedan. Susie would rest beneath the lawn where our kiddie pool kept us cool every summer before we headed indoors for our double-scoop ice cream cone. This was the same yard that Susie, in full spiritual armor, took on an enemy three times her size and survived.

I said, "Bye, Susie. I'm going to miss you very much, but I will love you forever." I turned away, tears spilling from my eyes, and went inside the house, straight to the yellow corded phone on our kitchen wall and dialed my grandmother. I don't remember my exact words, but the feeling I hold is my grandmother consoled me, which I have no doubt was two-fold. My Ava, the doggie salon pedicurist with a perpetual smile, needed consoling herself. Crying filled the silence between words.

Ava promised to check on me the next day. I went to my bedroom, got in bed, pulled the covers over my head, and bawled—with no warm little body beside me.

✦ ✦ ✦

WHEN CHRISTMAS ROLLED AROUND for the first time since Susie had passed, I carried on with our tree-decorating tradition, but I couldn't escape sadness. I had not been down this road before—Christmas without Susie. How was I going to get through it? My soul ached.

Pulling each tinsel branch out of the box, I imagined Susie sitting beside me on the floor. I hung her red felt Christmas stocking on the fireplace mantel in its usual place, in family order, as it had been done for the past sixteen years.

Susie symbolized the Christmas spirit. She accepted all people she met no matter what they looked like. She spread love and happiness wherever she went. She was holiday joy all year round.

On Christmas Day, after all the presents had been opened, I grabbed Susie's stocking and turned it upside down above the carpet, with the wrapped stocking-stuffer falling out. Once the rectangular goodie hit the floor, I opened it as I had normally done every Christmas with Susie sitting in front of me. I split the milk chocolate bar in two. I showed my dad, who was lounging in his recliner, and Mom and Ava sitting on the sofa, before I began my impromptu ceremony.

With one half of the milk chocolate bar in my left hand, arm resting in my lap, and the other half in my right hand, I raised it to the sky and said, "This is for you, Susie. We miss you so much. Even though you aren't sitting here with us, we know your spirit will always be around us. May Heaven's chocolate factory never break down, and may it crank out the tastiest treats for you around the clock. I'll see you later, Susie. Be sure to save half a bar for me."

LOVE LETTER

Dearest Susie,

Even though I loved you with all my heart, I don't think I fully appreciated the blessing God gave me until you were gone. You and I were just living, enjoying each other's company, exploring any chance we got, and comforting one another through our pain.

You taught me to be curious, to embrace possibility, to keep learning. You showed me unconditional love and loyalty, that true friends never leave your side. You instilled in me family first, always. You equipped me with a warrior's mindset—I win, not the bullies.

Our bond, strong from the moment we met, has been the key that unlocked who I came to be. As my first pet, you showed me the many ways an animal can beautify life. The lessons I learned from you shaped my every cell. My deep love for you, and all the animals that have graced my life, has led me to my work as an animal advocate. This passion gives me purpose and a profound joy that I may not have known if I didn't have you.

Our fifteen Christmases together have special meaning to me. I see you bouncing about the house, thrilled that tree-decorating day had finally come. I see you in your green, red, and white sweater, sitting by our tinsel tree on Christmas morning, waiting for the festivities to begin. And when Christmas day was over, I see you snuggling next to me in bed, energy spent, lulling me to sleep and guarding against nocturnal attack-rats.

I'm looking forward to the day I see that smile of yours again, Susie. I want to feel your soft, tan hair and hear your bark greeting me upon my arrival. You're probably up there in Heaven getting your toenails painted by Ava and being spoiled by her delightful treats. I can't wait to join in.

My wish is that our story inspires people to adopt a pet and experience what we had. I hope they see the benefits of a child growing up with the love of a pet. It's a friendship beyond compare.

Susie, thank you for choosing Mom and Dad, so you could be waiting at the door for me on my birthday.

You continue to be a sacred gift that influences every step I take. My life today is greater because I had a canine buddy who adored me from the moment we met.

Don't worry, Susie. I'm coming. You'll be at my side again someday, and we'll explore glorious Heaven together.

Love, Denise

ABOUT THE AUTHOR

Denise Lee Branco is the multi-award-winning author of *Rabbit at the Sliding Door: Chloe's Story* and *Horse at the Corner Post: Our Divine Journey*. Denise's passion is using her writing to highlight the human-animal bond and another to advocate for animal rescue. She is a member of the Dog Writers Association of America, Cat Writers Association, Northern California Publishers and Authors, Christian Indie Publishing Association, and other writing and publishing organizations. She has been a contributor to thirteen anthologies.

Denise is a passionate volunteer member of Pilots N Paws®, a 501(c)(3) non-profit organization involved with rescuing and transporting animals in need, and she is a Certified Pet Loss Specialist-Individual. She lives in the foothills of Northern California and loves leisure biking, foods with melted cheese, and spoiling her three rescued felines. To learn more about Denise, please visit www.DeniseInspiresYou.com.

ACKNOWLEDGMENTS

First and foremost, I wish to thank my parents for my devoted, pint-sized birthday gift with big brown eyes, four furry legs, and a curly tail. What a beautiful way for me to enter this world!

Writing about Susie and my childhood brought back so many special memories. I miss those days, Mom and Dad. I wish we could rewind the years and relive each moment. We can't, but this book can fill the void. It will always be my treasured keepsake to open and remind myself of your love for me and Susie, and the wonderful life on a ranch that you gave us.

Ava, I reaped the benefits of being your last grandchild. How lucky was I! You welcomed Susie and me into your home any time we wanted. I will always think back and laugh at the silly things we did or reminisce about the holidays that you made finer by being there.

Those memories of you will never fade. They are locked in my heart.

Loving thanks to my dear friend and editor, Valerie Ormond, for pushing, prodding, tugging, and praising as she helped me write Susie's story. Val, you didn't give up on me, and I'll never forget that. You always knew I could achieve excellence, and you didn't allow me to settle with mediocre writing. You brought out the best in me. This book is greater than I imagined because of you.

I am deeply grateful to Christine Horner, The Book Cover Whisperer, for designing another gorgeous book! Thank you, Christine, for helping me create a timeless tribute to Susie.

Heartfelt gratitude to my advance reviewers. I truly appreciate your time in reading Susie's story and supporting my endeavor. Your beautiful endorsements have touched me so.

The depth of my appreciation for the cherished people who buy my books is beyond what I can fully express. You keep me going with a burning desire to do better, give more, and make a difference. Thank you for blessing my life.

To the incredible team at Pilots N Paws, you have no idea how much your acceptance of my volunteer application earlier this year has meant to me. It has been the opportunity of a lifetime! My work for Pilots N Paws feeds my soul. It has immersed me deeper into my divine purpose by using my writing talents to promote animal rescue. To save a life gives me life. I am eternally grateful to be a Pilots N Paws volunteer.

Special thanks to my brothers and sisters in animal rescue. I appreciate all you do to help animals in need. You are the best of humanity! It is a tough job, and I am inspired by how you keep going, fighting back tears for the innocent victims and smiling in relief when they are finally safe. I'm honored to be a member of the pack!

I can't end without thanking Susie, Socks, Duckie, Brownie, Freedom, and all the other pets that graced my life growing up. You were the best gifts an only child could have. I never felt lonely with you there. Each of you made my days brighter. Heaven is going to be a lot of fun when we are all back together again!

Much Love,
Denise

RESOURCES

Article: Dog Ate Chocolate | Symptoms & Treatment of Chocolate Toxicity in Dogs: www.dogzhealth.com/dog-ate-chocolate/

History of Mercy Hospital, Merced California www.dignityhealth.org/central-california/locations/mercymedical-merced/about-us/history

Hill's: Facts and Personality Traits of Dog Breeds www.hillspet.com/dog-care/dog-breeds/dachshund www.hillspet.com/dog-care/dog-breeds/pekingese

American Kennel Club Breed Information: www.akc.org/dog-breeds/dachshund/ www.akc.org/dog-breeds/pekingese/

Pilots N Paws
4651 Howe Road, Landrum, SC 29356.
Visit www.pilotsnpaws.org

Rescued Pets are Wonderful Pekingese Rescue
P.O. Box 11336, Fort Lauderdale, FL 33339-1336.
Visit www.rescuedpekes.com

Canine Angels for Heaven—A Hospice Pet Sanctuary
W7530 Iroquois Trail, Delavan, WI 53115.
Visit www.canineangelsforheaven.org

Liz E's Pekingese Rescue
P.O. Box 687, Bull Shoals, AR, 72619.
Visit www.pekingesepatrol.com

Please remember to support your local animal rescues.

THANK YOU
for Reading
Dog at the Tinsel Tree: Susie's Story

HI, MY NAME IS SUSIE, writing to you from beautiful Heaven. Thank you for reading my story. Since this book is dedicated to me, it would mean so much if you left a book review on an online bookstore. A portion of sales will be donated to animal rescue organizations. So, the more books purchased, the more animals we can help.

Thanks again for making a difference in the lives of animals all over the world.

OTHER BOOKS
by the Author

HORSE AT THE CORNER POST:
Our Divine Journey

✦ ✦ **Silver Medal Award Winner** ✦ ✦

HAVE YOU EVER EXPERIENCED an unexplainable connection with your pet? Shared a language all your own that could only astound others? When the day came for your dear pet to return to Heaven, was your bond so strong that it took every ounce of your soul to let go?

Horse at the Corner Post by Denise Lee Branco is a three-decade-long true story that epitomizes the power of a spiritual bond of love between two best friends—one, two-legged; the other, four. *Horse at the Corner Post* reminds us all of the unconditional love animals give, and the immeasurable joy they bring to our lives.

✦ ✦ ✦

Now Available at All Leading
Booksellers & Online eBook Distributors

RABBIT AT THE SLIDING DOOR: Chloe's Story

✦ ✦ Winner of 14 Book Awards! ✦ ✦

WHEN AN UNEXPECTED VISITOR arrives at Denise's sliding door one summer morning, she had no idea her life was about to change forever. She found a Palomino in her backyard—not the kind she ever thought she'd see in suburbia or that she needed—with a fluffy white tail and a twitchy pink nose.

For her own safety, this abandoned rabbit could no longer be free range. Denise and Chloe's journey takes them both through harrowing situations to a reunion with the promise of protection, devotion, and serenity.

Rabbit at the Sliding Door is the touching story of how companionship and love come in all forms and lessons can be learned from every life. What would you do if a rabbit showed up at your door?

✦ ✦ ✦

Now Available at All Leading
Booksellers & Online eBook Distributors

www.ingramcontent.com/pod-product-compliance
Lightning Source LLC
Chambersburg PA
CBHW062112290426
44110CB00023B/2786